meet *Emilie Richards*

Photo by Creation Waits

*N*ow a USA TODAY bestselling author of women's fiction, Emilie Richards recalls fondly the months she served as a VISTA volunteer in the Arkansas Ozarks.

"This was the country's third poorest county," Emilie said in an interview from her Virginia home. "They had no phones, no safe water supply and no indoor plumbing. But the women created beauty out of nothing—turning scraps of old clothing and feedsacks into exquisitely beautiful quilts."

Emilie said the women insisted she quilt with them in the evenings, "and then later, they'd take out my stitches," she laughingly recalls of her early attempts at the craft.

The 20-year-old college student was left with a richness of experience and a love of quilting that would forever change her life and ultimately inspire a series of novels about the age-old craft. Emilie went on to finish her undergraduate degree in American studies and her master's in family development. She served as a therapist in a mental health center, as a parent services coordinator for Head Start families and in several pastoral counseling centers. Now a full-time writer, Emilie has drawn on these experiences while crafting more than 50 books.

In *Wedding Ring*, the first Shenandoah Album novel, Emilie uses the stages of quilting as a metaphor for the cycles of marriage. In *Endless Chain*, quilting serves as an activity that binds a community together in two parallel stories about human rights. In the third Shenandoah Album novel, *Lover's Knot*, an heirloom quilt bridges generations to help a young man uncover the past and find the key to his future. Three pattern books, *Quilt Along with Emilie Richards—Wedding Ring*, *Endless Chain*, and *Lover's Knot*, offer Emilie's fans a chance to create their own versions of the quilts in her novels.

To learn more about Emilie, visit her Web site at www.emilierichards.com.

LEISURE ARTS. INC.
Little Rock, Arkansas

Read the books that *Inspired* the projects

Leisure Arts is pleased to offer these quilting instruction books as companions to Emilie's compelling stories.

Quilt Along with Emilie Richards: Wedding Ring includes complete instructions for creating eight quilts from the story, while *Quilt Along with Emilie Richards: Endless Chain* is a collection of six quilts like those made by the inhabitants of Toms Brook.

And now we present a third pattern book to inspire your creativity. *Quilt Along with Emilie Richards: Lover's Knot* offers six traditional quilt designs, including Log Cabin, Cactus Bloom, Churn Dash, Big Dipper, Antique Basket, and Lover's Knot. You'll also find Helen's Signature Blocks.

Enhanced with excerpts from the novels, each quilting book gives the reader a glimpse of the unforgettable characters created by the gifted author.

Now there are three exciting novels in Emilie Richards' *Shenandoah Album* Series, *Wedding Ring*, *Endless Chain*, and *Lover's Knot*. Each is rich with family drama, romance — and quilts!

Read Emilie Richards' *Shenandoah Album* novels, then quilt along with the women of Toms Brook and Fitch Crossing Road. You may just discover a lifelong passion of your very own!

meet the characters from
Lover's Knot

kendra taylor

After narrowly escaping death, newspaper journalist Kendra Taylor retreats to a cabin nestled in Virginia's Shenandoah Valley to heal and sort out her feelings about her troubled marriage. The land was bequeathed to her husband by a maternal grandmother he never knew, and the cabin has been abandoned for years.

As she is welcomed into the rural community of Toms Brook, Kendra becomes curious about an heirloom Lover's Knot quilt, which is another piece of Isaac's unexplored past. The unusual quilt clearly has a story to tell, and Kendra is convinced that helping her husband connect with his roots might help him reconnect with her, as well.

"Kendra had spent very little time asking herself why the carjacking had happened to her. She didn't expect favoritism from God, but she had asked herself how she had let anger at Isaac lead her into that dark parking lot when she had been too sick to fend for herself. The answer didn't please her. The night she'd been shot she had set out to prove something. By doing so, she had set a chain of events in motion."
—from Lover's Knot

helen henry

In Toms Brook, Virginia, the unrivaled expert on quilts is Helen Henry, a forthright woman of senior years. Helen is well known for her stubbornness and independence, yet she owns a keen insight into the hearts of others. When Helen learns that Kendra has moved into Leah's old cabin to recover from an injury, the elderly woman takes a special interest in helping the young reporter. For if there's anything that Helen knows well, it's the healing power of quilts.

leah blackburn

After her parents died in 1932, almost every eligible bachelor in the county came calling on seventeen-year-old Leah Blackburn. Knowing that she and her frail sister, Birdie, couldn't manage the farm themselves, Leah understood that she must marry soon. But Jesse Spurlock was the only man that Leah wanted, and he hadn't bothered to visit her at all. With her thoughts so preoccupied, Leah paid little attention to rumors that the United States Government planned to build a park in the mountains of Virginia. Yet it would soon became apparent that the Blackburns, Spurlocks, and all their neighbors were in danger of losing their beloved homes.

birdie blackburn

Birdie Blackburn had always believed in signs and omens. They helped her make sense of a world that had not been kind to her. In 1919, poliomyelitis had come calling in the mountains of Virginia, and it left eight-year-old Birdie with a crippled leg and a body that into maturity remained weak as a child's. But Birdie's mother had carefully taught her to cook and sew, skills that didn't require strong legs. When her sister, Leah, became engaged, Birdie made a Lover's Knot quilt for her wedding gift. With the promise of happiness surrounding their little family, no one could foresee the darkness that lay ahead, not even Birdie.

"Birdie was beautiful. She had black hair that fell in thick waves to her shoulders. Her eyes were as blue as a June sky, and her skin was clear and rosy. Perhaps it was her poor vision, or perhaps only the way she viewed life, but Birdie always appeared to be staring into the distance."
—from Lover's Knot

As a passionate story of strength, loss and desperation unfolds, the secrets of two quilts are revealed and the threads of an unraveling marriage are secured. In the rich, evocative prose that earned high praise for Wedding Ring and Endless Chain, Emilie Richards crafts the third tale in the Shenandoah Album series, resonant with the power of love and family ties.

Lover's Knot Quilt

Birdie's wedding gift to Leah was a breathtaking Lover's Knot quilt made from feedsack fabrics. Here, reproduction fabrics were used to match the description of Birdie's beautifully finished gift. And it is gracefully echo-quilted along the diagonal curves, drawing the viewer's eye across the quilt to give the impression of gentle movement. Many decades after Leah's wedding, Kendra's husband inherits a Lover's Knot quilt from Leah—but his heirloom quilt is finished in a most peculiar way.

FINISHED QUILT SIZE: 85" x 85" (216 cm x 216 cm)
FINISHED BLOCK SIZE: 12" x 12" (30 cm x 30 cm)

CUTTING OUT THE PIECES

*Follow **Rotary Cutting**, page 50, to cut fabric. All measurements include a ¹/₄" seam allowance. Refer to **Template Cutting**, page 50, to use templates, page 11.*

From white solid:
- Cut 10 strips 2"w. From these strips, cut 196 **squares** 2" x 2".
- Cut 196 pieces using template **A**.
- Cut 98 pieces using template **B**.

From assorted red prints:
- Cut 9 sets of 4 matching **squares** 2" x 2".
- Cut 9 sets of 4 matching pieces using template **A**.
- Cut 9 sets of 2 matching pieces using template **B**.

From assorted purple prints:
- Cut 16 sets of 4 matching **squares** 2" x 2".
- Cut 16 sets of 4 matching pieces using template **A**.
- Cut 16 sets of 2 matching pieces using template **B**.

From assorted green prints:
- Cut 16 sets of 4 matching **squares** 2" x 2".
- Cut 16 sets of 4 matching pieces using template **A**.
- Cut 16 sets of 2 matching pieces using template **B**.

From assorted blue prints:
- Cut 8 sets of 4 matching **squares** 2" x 2".
- Cut 8 sets of 4 matching pieces using template **A**.
- Cut 8 sets of 2 matching pieces using template **B**.

"Birdie stayed up late every night quilting and finishing one of the two Lover's Knot quilt tops for Leah's marriage bed."
— from Lover's Knot

YARDAGE REQUIREMENTS

Yardage is based on 43"/44" (109 cm/112 cm) wide fabric.

7¹/₈ yds (6.5 m) of white solid fabric (includes binding)

1¹/₂ yds (1.4 m) **total** of assorted red print fabrics

2¹/₄ yds (2.1 m) **total** of assorted purple print fabrics

2¹/₄ yds (2.1 m) **total** of assorted green print fabrics

1¹/₄ yds (1.1 m) **total** of assorted blue print fabrics

7³/₄ yds (7.1 m) of backing fabric

You will also need: 93" x 93" (236 cm x 236 cm) square of batting

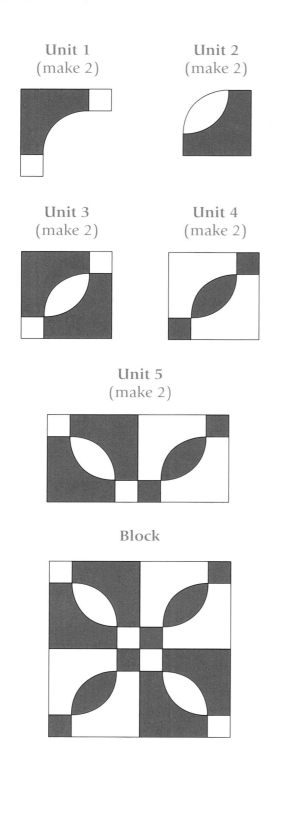

Unit 1
(make 2)

Unit 2
(make 2)

Unit 3
(make 2)

Unit 4
(make 2)

Unit 5
(make 2)

Block

ASSEMBLING THE QUILT TOP

*Follow **Piecing and Pressing**, page 51, and refer to **Quilt Top Diagram** to assemble the quilt top. **Note:** For each block you will need, 4 A's, 2 B's, and 4 squares from a matching print and white solid fabrics.*

1. Sew 1 red print **A** and 2 white solid **squares** together to make **Unit 1**. Make 2 **Unit 1's**.

2. *(**Note:** To sew curved seams in Steps 2 and 3, match center marks. Pin at center and at each end, then match and pin between pins. Sew seam with **B** on bottom next to feed dogs. Press seam allowance toward **B**.)* Sew 1 matching red print **A** and 1 white solid **B** together to make **Unit 2**. Make 2 **Unit 2's**.

3. Sew 1 **Unit 1** and 1 **Unit 2** together to make **Unit 3**. Make 2 **Unit 3's**.

4. Repeat **Steps 1-3** using 2 matching red print **squares**, 2 white solid **A's**, and 1 red print **B** to make **Unit 4**. Make 2 **Unit 4's**.

5. Sew 1 **Unit 3** and 1 **Unit 4** together to make **Unit 5**. Make 2 **Unit 5's**.

6. Sew 2 **Unit 5's** together to make **Block**.

7. Repeat **Steps 1-6** to make 9 assorted **red print blocks**, 16 assorted **purple print blocks**, 16 assorted **green print blocks**, and 8 assorted **blue print blocks**.

8. Sew 4 assorted green print blocks, 2 assorted blue print blocks, and 1 assorted purple print block together to make **Row 1**. Make 2 **Row 1's**.

9. Sew 2 assorted blue print blocks, 2 assorted green print blocks, 2 assorted purple print blocks, and 1 assorted red print block together to make **Row 2**. Make 2 **Row 2's**.

10. Sew 2 assorted green print blocks, 3 assorted purple print blocks, and 2 assorted red print blocks together to make **Row 3**. Make 2 **Row 3's**.

11. Sew 4 assorted purple print blocks and 3 assorted red print blocks together to make **Row 4**.

12. Sew **Rows** together to make **Quilt Top**.

COMPLETING THE QUILT TOP

1. Follow **Quilting,** page 54, to mark, layer, and quilt as desired. Refer to photo, page 11, for a close-up of quilting design.

2. Cut a 30" square of binding fabric. Follow **Making Continuous Bias Binding**, page 60, to make $9^{7}/_{8}$ yds of $2^{1}/_{4}$"w binding.

3. Follow **Attaching Binding With Mitered Corners**, page 61, to bind quilt.

Quilt Top Diagram

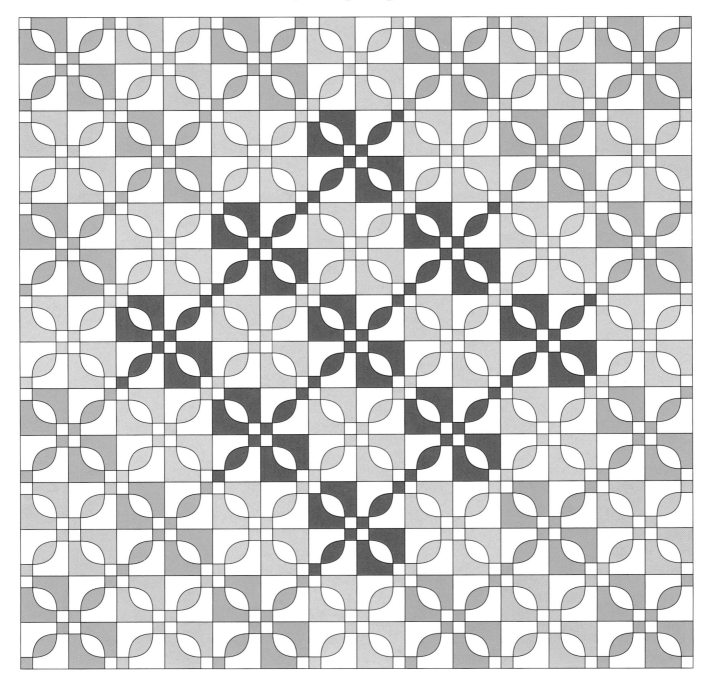

"*Kendra had begun collecting antique quilts more than a year ago, but the Lover's Knot was her favorite. She knew little about it, only that Leah had done her best to ensure that the quilt would make its way to the grandson she had never known.*

The quilt was double bed size and not an inch more. Although the color choices, scrap prints of greens, blues, purples and reds, were lovely, two things set the quilt apart.

The first were signatures, all neatly embroidered but scattered over the surface as if they'd been sprinkled at random. The other was the quilting itself. Quilts of the era had often been stitched with parallel intersecting lines or half circles. Accomplished quilters had added complicated feathers and wreaths, vines or flowers. The Lover's Knot quilt had lines that meandered with no discernible pattern or plan."

— from Lover's Knot

10

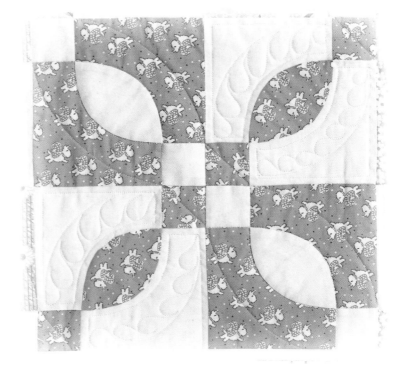

"'*This here's what they call a conversation print,*' Helen said. '*See the little houses, the animals? Some good old prints in this quilt. And there was an eye for color. A lot of trouble went into choosing them. See the way the colors fan out? Reds in the center, purples moving into blues until we get these greens at the border? Scrap quilt yes, but planning went into it.*'"
— from Lover's Knot

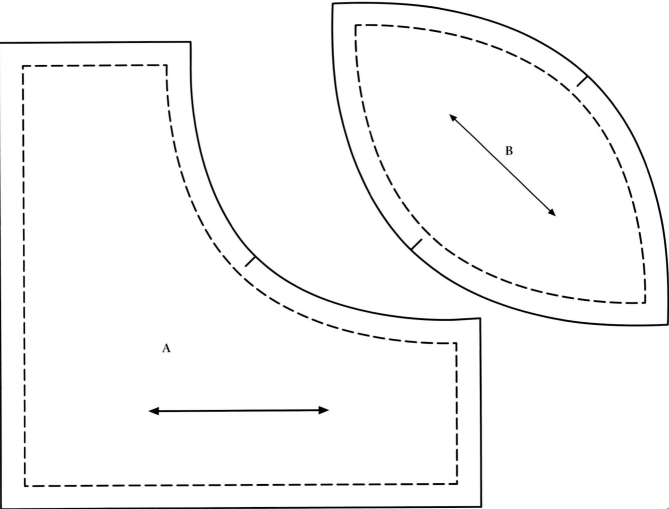

A

B

Helen's Signature Blocks

Does anything make a quilter's fingers itch to stitch more than a set of pretty blocks, all ready to be joined? Helen is hoping that Kendra will "catch the itch" and make a quilt using the signature blocks she gave the younger woman.

FINISHED BLOCK SIZE: 12" x 12" (30 cm x 30 cm)

Make as many of these signature blocks as you desire using any combination of fabrics. You can make all the blocks the same or mix them up for a sampler signature quilt. Simply set your blocks together with sashings and sashing squares (if desired) and add a border to make a beautiful wall hanging, throw, or bed size quilt.

MEMORY BLOCK

Cutting Out The Pieces

From muslin:
- Cut 1 **square** $4^1/_2$" x $4^1/_2$".

From blue print:
- Cut 8 **squares** $2^1/_2$" x $2^1/_2$".

From pink print:
- Cut 4 **rectangles** $2^1/_2$" x $4^1/_2$".
- Cut 4 **squares** $2^1/_2$" x $2^1/_2$".

From red print:
- Cut 8 **small squares** $2^1/_2$" x $2^1/_2$".
- Cut 4 **large squares** $2^7/_8$" x $2^7/_8$".

From brown print:
- Cut 4 **small squares** $2^1/_2$" x $2^1/_2$".
- Cut 4 **large squares** $2^7/_8$" x $2^7/_8$".
- Cut 4 **rectangles** $2^1/_2$" x $4^1/_2$".

YARDAGE REQUIREMENTS

Yardage for blocks will vary since any number of blocks and any color combinations may be used. For our blocks we used fat quarters. A fat quarter measures approximately 18" x 22" (46 cm x 56 cm).

CUTTING AND ASSEMBLING THE BLOCKS

*Follow **Rotary Cutting**, page 50, to cut fabric. All measurements include a $^1/_4$" seam allowance. Follow **Piecing and Pressing**, page 51, to assemble the blocks.*

"The meeting began with a show and tell, and Kendra showed the signature blocks Helen had given her. The group discussed the best placement and what kind of sashing to use between blocks. Despite herself, Kendra was almost enthused about some of the possibilities."

— from Lover's Knot

Making The Block

1. Draw a diagonal line on wrong side of each brown print **large square**. With right sides together, place 1 brown print **large square** on top of 1 red print **large square**. Stitch seam ¹/₄" from each side of drawn line (**Fig. 1**).

2. Cut along drawn line and press seam allowances to darker fabric to make 2 **Triangle-Squares**. Make 8 **Triangle-Squares**.

3. With right sides together, place 1 blue print **square** on 1 end of 1 pink print **rectangle** and stitch diagonally. Trim ¹/₄" from stitching line (**Fig. 2**). Open up and press, pressing seam allowances to darker fabric.

4. Place another blue print **square** on opposite end of **rectangle**. Stitch and trim as shown in **Fig. 3**. Open up and press to complete **Flying Geese Unit 1**. Make 4 **Flying Geese Unit 1's**.

5. Repeat **Steps 3-4** using red print **small squares** and brown print **rectangles** to make 4 **Flying Geese Unit 2's**.

6. Sew 2 brown print **small squares**, 2 **Triangle-Squares**, and 1 **Flying Geese Unit 2** together to make **Unit 1**. **Make 2 Unit 1's**.

7. Sew 2 **Triangle-Squares**, 2 pink print **squares**, and 1 **Flying Geese Unit 1** together to make **Unit 2**. **Make 2 Unit 2's**.

8. Sew 2 **Flying Geese Unit 2's**, 2 **Flying Geese Unit 1's**, and **muslin square** together to make **Unit 3**.

9. Sew **Unit 1's**, **Unit 2's**, and **Unit 3** together to make **Block**.

Fig. 1

Triangle-Squares
(make 8)

Fig. 2

Fig. 3

Flying Geese Unit 1
(make 4)

Flying Geese Unit 2
(make 4)

Unit 1
(make 2)

Unit 2
(make 2)

Unit 3

Block

"It's true any pattern can be a friendship quilt, as long as there's some place in the block light enough to sign or embroider."

— Helen Henry

Fig. 1

Triangle-Squares
(make 20)

Unit 1
(make 2)

Unit 2
(make 2)

CHIMNEY SWEEP BLOCK

Cutting Out The Pieces
From muslin:
- Cut 1 **rectangle** $2^3/_8$" x $6^1/_8$".
- Cut 2 **squares** $2^3/_8$" x $2^3/_8$".

From brown print fabric:
- Cut 4 **small squares** $2^3/_8$" x $2^3/_8$".
- Cut 10 **large squares** $2^7/_8$" x $2^7/_8$".

From pink print fabric:
- Cut 2 squares $4^7/_8$" x $4^7/_8$". Cut each square once diagonally to make a total of 4 **triangles**.
- Cut 10 squares $2^7/_8$" x $2^7/_8$".

Making The Block
1. Draw a diagonal line on wrong side of each pink print **square**. With right sides together, place 1 pink print **square** on top of 1 brown print **large square**. Stitch seam $1/_4$" from each side of drawn line (**Fig. 1**).

2. Cut along drawn line and press seam allowances to darker fabric to make 2 **Triangle-Squares**. Make 20 **Triangle-Squares**.

3. Sew 4 **Triangle-Squares** together to make **Unit 1**. Make 2 **Unit 1's**.

4. Sew 6 **Triangle-Squares** together to make **Unit 2**. Make 2 **Unit 2's**.

5. Sew 2 brown print **small squares** and 1 muslin **square** together to make **Unit 3**. Make 2 **Unit 3's**.

6. Sew 2 **Unit 3's** and muslin **rectangle** together to make **Unit 4**.

7. Sew 1 **triangle** to each side of Unit 4 to make **Unit 5**.

8. Sew 1 **Unit 1** to opposite sides of Unit 5 to make **Unit 6**.

9. Sew 1 **Unit 2** to each remaining side of Unit 6 to make **Block**.

Unit 3
(make 2)

Unit 4

Unit 5

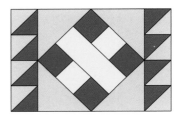

Unit 6

Block

"Kendra slipped a thimble Helen had provided on her third finger. It felt like a lead weight. She tried waving her thimbled finger, just to see if she could. Privately, Kendra thought her thimbled finger and thumb were going to need a stiff drink, a relaxing soak in a tub, and at least six ounces of chocolate."

— from Lover's Knot

Fig. 1

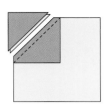

Fig. 2

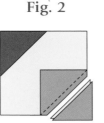

Unit 1
(make 2)

Unit 2
(make 4)

Unit 3
(make 2)

Unit 4
(make 2)

Block

ARKANSAS CROSSROADS BLOCK

Cutting Out The Pieces

From muslin:
- Cut 2 **squares** $6^1/_2$" x $6^1/_2$".

From red print:
- Cut 4 **squares** $3^1/_2$" x $3^1/_2$".

From pink print:
- Cut 4 **squares** $3^1/_2$" x $3^1/_2$".

From brown print:
- Cut 4 **squares** $3^1/_2$" x $3^1/_2$".

Making The Block

1. With right sides together, place 1 red print **square** on 1 corner of 1 muslin **square** and stitch diagonally. Trim $^1/_4$" from stitching line (**Fig. 1**). Open up and press seam allowances to darker fabric.

2. Place 1 red print **square** on opposite corner of muslin **square** and stitch diagonally. Trim $^1/_4$" from stitching line (**Fig. 2**). Open up and press to complete **Unit 1**. Make 2 **Unit 1's**.

3. Sew 1 brown print **square** and 1 pink print **square** together to make **Unit 2**. Make 4 **Unit 2's**.

4. Sew 2 **Unit 2's** together to make **Unit 3**. Make 2 **Unit 3's**.

5. Sew 1 **Unit 1** and 1 **Unit 3** together to make **Unit 4**. Make 2 **Unit 4's**.

6. Sew 2 **Unit 4's** together to make **Block**.

SIGNATURE CHAIN BLOCK

Cutting Out The Pieces

From muslin:
- Cut 1 **large rectangle** $4^1/_2$" x $8^1/_2$".
- Cut 2 **small rectangles** $2^1/_2$" x $4^1/_2$".

From red print:
- Cut 6 **squares** $2^1/_2$" x $2^1/_2$".

From blue print:
- Cut 6 **squares** $2^1/_2$" x $2^1/_2$".

From pink print:
- Cut 4 **rectangles** $2^1/_2$" x $4^1/_2$".
- Cut 4 **squares** $2^1/_2$" x $2^1/_2$".

Making The Block

1. Sew 2 pink print **rectangles**, 1 blue print **square**, and 1 red print **square** together to make **Unit 1**. Make 2 **Unit 1's**.

2. Sew 2 pink print **squares**, 1 red print **square**, 1 blue print **square**, and 1 muslin **small rectangle** together to make **Unit 2**. Make 2 **Unit 2's**.

3. Sew 1 red print **square** and 1 blue print **square** together to make **Unit 3**. Make 2 **Unit 3's**.

4. Sew 1 **Unit 3** to each short end of muslin **large rectangle** to make **Unit 4**.

5. Sew **Unit 1's**, **Unit 2's**, and **Unit 4** together to make **Block**.

Unit 1
(make 2)

Unit 2
(make 2)

Unit 3
(make 2)

Unit 4

Block

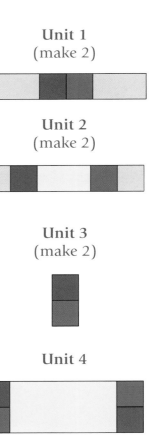

Unit 1

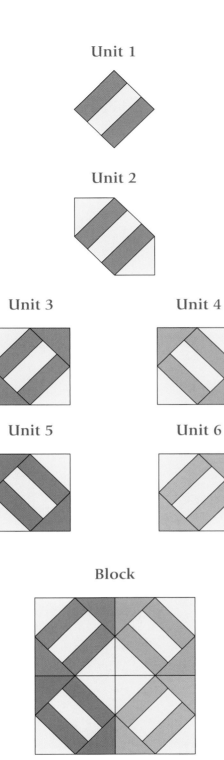

Unit 2

Unit 3   Unit 4

Unit 5   Unit 6

Block

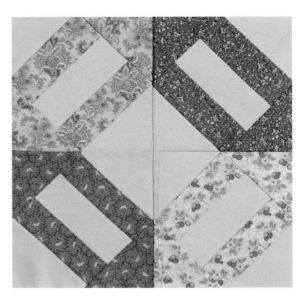

CRACKER BLOCK

Cutting Out The Pieces
From muslin:
- Cut 4 squares $3^7/_8$" x $3^7/_8$". Cut each square once diagonally to make a total of 8 **triangles**.
- Cut 4 **rectangles** 2" x $4^3/_4$".

From *each* of 2 brown and 2 pink prints:
- Cut 1 square $3^7/_8$" x $3^7/_8$". Cut square once diagonally to make a total of 2 **triangles**.
- Cut 2 **rectangles** $1^7/_8$" x $4^3/_4$".

Making The Block
1. Sew 2 pink print **rectangles** and 1 muslin **rectangle** together to make **Unit 1**.

2. Sew 1 muslin **triangle** to opposite sides of Unit 1 to make **Unit 2**.

3. Sew 1 pink print **triangle** to each remaining side of Unit 2 to make **Unit 3**.

4. Repeat **Steps 1-3** using muslin **rectangles** and **triangles** and matching print **rectangles** and **triangles** to make **Units 4-6**.

5. Sew **Unit 3**, **Unit 4**, **Unit 5**, and **Unit 6** together to make **Block**.

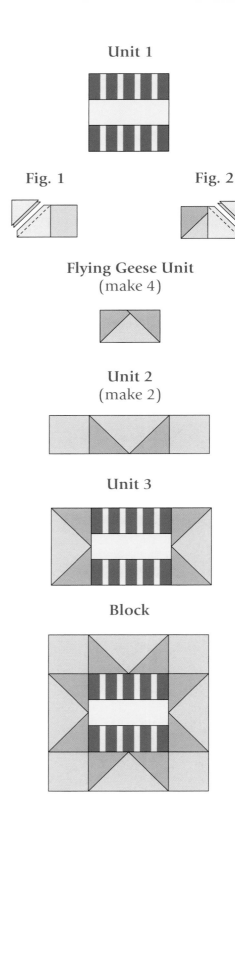

Unit 1

Fig. 1   Fig. 2

Flying Geese Unit
(make 4)

Unit 2
(make 2)

Unit 3

Block

SIGNATURE STAR BLOCK

Cutting Out The Pieces

From muslin:
- Cut 1 **rectangle** $2^1/_2$" x $6^1/_2$".

From blue stripe:
- Cut 2 **rectangles** $2^1/_2$" x $6^1/_2$".

From blue print:
- Cut 8 **squares** $3^1/_2$" x $3^1/_2$".

From pink print:
- Cut 4 **rectangles** $3^1/_2$" x $6^1/_2$".
- Cut 4 **squares** $3^1/_2$" x $3^1/_2$".

Making The Block

1. Sew 2 blue stripe **rectangles** and 1 muslin **rectangle** together to make **Unit 1**.

2. With right sides together, place 1 blue print **square** on 1 end of 1 pink print **rectangle** and stitch diagonally. Trim $1/_4$" from stitching line (**Fig. 1**). Open up and press, pressing seam allowance to darker fabric.

3. Place another blue print **square** on opposite end of **rectangle**. Stitch and trim as shown in **Fig. 2**. Open up and press to complete **Flying Geese Unit**. Make 4 **Flying Geese Units**.

4. Sew 1 pink print **square** to each end of 1 Flying Geese Unit to make **Unit 2**. Make 2 **Unit 2's**.

5. Sew 1 **Flying Geese Unit** to opposite sides of Unit 1 to make **Unit 3**.

6. Sew **Unit 2's** to **Unit 3** to make **Block**.

Why Album Quilts?

Another popular use for album quilts was fundraising. It was common for church groups and other organizations to raise money for charity by creating signature quilts. The signatures on these quilts are not those of the creators, but of the persons who made contributions to the fund. There were no limits to the number of signatures a fundraising quilt might have. This is why Helen Henry tells Kendra Taylor that her Churn Dash quilt, with so many names on it, must have been a fundraiser. The Cactus Bloom quilt, on the other hand, was not an album quilt at all. It served its charitable function simply by being raffled at a social event.

You may have noticed the absence of signatures on our "album" quilts, as well as Helen's Signature Blocks. That's because the Churn Dash and Big Dipper quilts are genuine antiques that we did not wish to alter, while the Lover's Knot quilt, Log Cabin quilt, and Helen's Signature Blocks were created especially for this publication. If you decide to use one of our patterns to make an album quilt, we recommend having each participant embroider their name or message on their block. Need more convenience? Sign the blocks with fine-point permanent fabric markers, instead. Whether stitched by one quilter or produced by a group of friends, any of these designs will yield a quilt that will be cherished for decades to come.

Whether signed with love or fashioned as a means to reach a common goal, album quilts of the nineteenth and early twentieth centuries played an important part in cementing bonds between friends, neighbors, and family members.

Also known as *friendship* or *signature* quilts, album quilts were created by groups of women (with the occasional male contributor) who worked together to make quilts for individuals experiencing a significant life change. These milestone occasions included, among others: marriage, the arrival of a new baby, or a move across a great distance.

Each person who took part in creating an album quilt signed her name to the block or other quilt piece she contributed. These signatures were either signed in ink or embroidered. And because such a quilt was typically composed of clothing scraps, the recipient would also be reminded of the persons who wore the original garments— making it a very sentimental gift, indeed! When it was time to present the results of this group effort, it wasn't always in the form of a finished quilt. Sometimes just the blocks or top were given with the intention of holding a group event to finish the quilt.

Basket Quilt

This Basket quilt has seen the turn of two centuries, and it's easy to imagine it being part of Kendra's collection. Although its faded colors indicate it was often used for warmth, this album quilt is otherwise in fair condition and must have been cherished through the years. Permanent ink may have been difficult to find in the late 1800s; the signatures bled into the surrounding fabric until most of the names are illegible.

FINISHED QUILT SIZE: 75″ x 88″ (191 cm x 224 cm)
FINISHED BLOCK SIZE: 10″ x 10″ (25 cm x 25 cm)

CUTTING OUT THE PIECES

*Follow **Rotary Cutting**, page 50, to cut fabric. All strips are cut across the width of the fabric unless otherwise noted. Cutting lengths given for borders and long sashing strips are exact. All measurements include a $1/4$" seam allowance.*

From tan solid:
- Cut 4 strips $8^7/_8$"w. From these strips, cut 15 squares $8^7/_8$" x $8^7/_8$". Cut each square in half once diagonally to make 30 **triangles (A)**.
- Cut 2 strips $4^7/_8$"w. From these strips, cut 15 squares $4^7/_8$" x $4^7/_8$". Cut each square in half once diagonally to make 30 **triangles (B)**.
- Cut 10 strips $2^1/_2$"w. From these strips, cut 60 **rectangles** $2^1/_2$" x $6^1/_2$ **(C)**.

From *each* fabric No. 1:
- Cut 1 bias strip for **basket handle** $1^1/_4$" x 11".
- Cut 6 **squares** $2^7/_8$" x $2^7/_8$" **(D)**. Cut 3 of the D squares in half once diagonally to make 6 **triangles (E)**.

From *each* fabric No. 2:
- Cut 3 **squares** $2^7/_8$" x $2^7/_8$" **(D)**.
- Cut 1 **square** $2^1/_2$" x $2^1/_2$" **(F)**.

From brown solid:
- Cut 2 *lengthwise* **top** and **bottom inner borders** $2^1/_2$" x $74^1/_2$".
- Cut 2 *lengthwise* **side inner borders** $2^1/_2$" x $75^1/_2$".
- Cut 2 *lengthwise* **top** and **bottom outer borders** $2^1/_2$" x $74^1/_2$".
- Cut 2 *lengthwise* **side outer borders** $2^1/_2$" x $75^1/_2$".
- Cut 8 *lengthwise* **long sashing strips** $1^1/_2$" x $75^1/_2$".
- Cut 50 **short sashing strips** $1^1/_2$" x $10^1/_2$".

From green print:
- Cut 2 *lengthwise* **top** and **bottom middle borders** $2^1/_2$" x $74^1/_2$".
- Cut 2 *lengthwise* **side middle borders** $2^1/_2$" x $75^1/_2$".
- Cut 4 *lengthwise* **long sashing strips** $1^1/_2$" x $75^1/_2$".
- Cut 25 **short sashing strips** $1^1/_2$" x $10^1/_2$".

"Helen thumbed through the rest of Kendra's quilts. 'Well, these others are pretty, all right. This Basket quilt's a real keeper, even if it's worn at the edges.'"
—from Lover's Knot

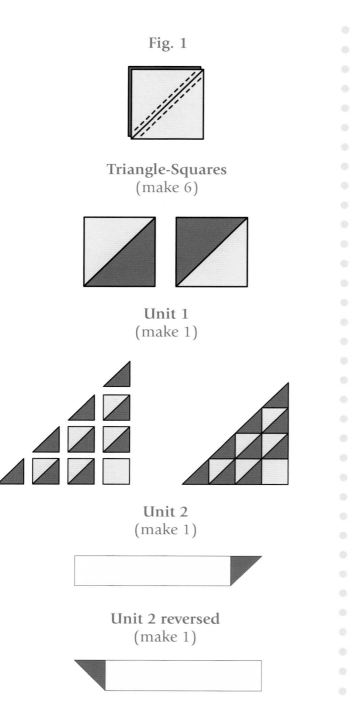

Fig. 1

Triangle-Squares
(make 6)

Unit 1
(make 1)

Unit 2
(make 1)

Unit 2 reversed
(make 1)

ASSEMBLING THE QUILT TOP

*Follow **Piecing and Pressing**, page 51, to assemble the quilt top.*

1. Draw a diagonal line on wrong side of each fabric No. 1 **square (D)**. With right sides together, place 1 fabric No. 1 **square (D)** on top of 1 fabric No. 2 **square (D)**. Stitch seam $^1/_4$" from each side of drawn line **(Fig. 1)**

2. Cut along drawn line and press seam allowances to darker fabric to make 2 **Triangle-Squares**. Make 6 **Triangle-Squares**. Discard 1 Triangle-Square.

3. Refer to **Unit 1 Diagram** to sew 5 **Triangle-Squares**, 4 **E's**, and 1 **F** into **Rows**. Sew Rows together to make **Unit 1**.

4. Referring to **Unit 2 Diagram** for orientation, sew 1 **E** and 1 **C** together to make 1 **Unit 2** and 1 **Unit 2 reversed**.

"'I do not know a remedy for keeping the government of Virginia away from these mountains. I surely wish I did. I am sorry the gentlemen at Skyland think the government stealing what belongs to us is a good idea.'"
—Leah Blackburn

5. Refer to **Unit 3 Diagram** to sew **Unit 2**, **Unit 2 reversed** and 1 B to **Unit 1** to make **Unit 3**.

6. Referring to **Unit 4 Diagram** for placement and following **Needle-Turn Appliqué**, page 52, appliqué 1 **basket handle** to A to make **Unit 4**.

7. Sew **Unit 3** and **Unit 4** together to complete **Basket Block**. Repeat **Steps 1-6** to make a total of 30 **Basket Blocks**.

8. Sew 1 green and 2 brown **short sashing strips** together to make a **Short Sashing Unit**. Make 25 **Short Sashing Units**.

9. Sew 1 green and 2 brown **long sashing strips** together to make a **Long Sashing Unit**. Make 4 **Long Sashing Units**.

10. Refer to **Assembly Diagram**, page 26, to sew 6 **Basket Blocks** and 5 **Short Sashing Units** into **Vertical Rows**. Make 5 Vertical Rows. Keeping horizontal sashing strips aligned, sew **Rows** together with **Long Sashing Units** to complete center section of **Quilt Top**.

11. Referring to **Assembly Diagram**, page 26, sew **inner**, **middle**, and **outer Side Borders** together. Repeat for remaining **inner**, **middle**, and **outer Side Borders**. Sew **Side Borders** to center section of **Quilt Top**.

12. Sew **inner**, **middle**, and **outer Top Borders** together. Repeat for **Bottom Border**. Sew **Top** and **Bottom Borders** to center section of **Quilt Top**.

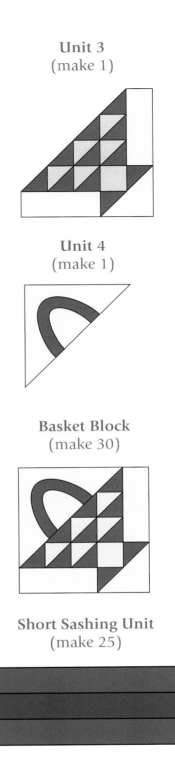

Unit 3
(make 1)

Unit 4
(make 1)

Basket Block
(make 30)

Short Sashing Unit
(make 25)

COMPLETING THE QUILT TOP

1. Follow **Quilting,** page 54, to mark, layer, and quilt as desired.
    Our quilt is hand quilted with overlapping circles in the
    blocks, diagonal lines in the sashings, and a fan pattern in
    the borders.

2. Cut a 31" square of binding fabric. Follow **Making Continuous
    Bias Binding**, page 60, to make $9\frac{1}{2}$ yds of $2\frac{1}{2}$"w binding.

3. Follow **Attaching Binding With Mitered Corners**, page 61, to
    bind quilt. *Note: The corners of this quilt appear slightly rounded,
    but for ease of construction, our instructions call for mitered corners.*

Assembly Diagram

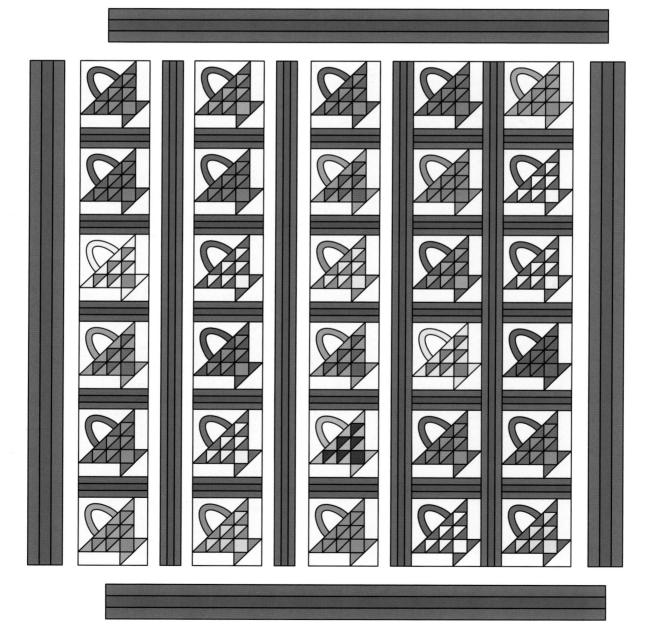

"'You got the quilt bug, you know, only you're looking at things from the outside in. I'm fixing to change that.'"

—Helen Henry to Kendra Taylor

Big Dipper Quilt

Do you see the stars dancing across this pink-and-white quilt? If you want to see your Big Dipper quilt really sparkle, try using a mix of light fabrics for the "stars" and dark fabrics for the "sky." The antique quilt pictured has an irregular scalloped border, however our pattern has been modified to make the scalloped border symmetrical.

FINISHED QUILT SIZE: 78¹/₂" x 78¹/₂" (199 cm x 199 cm)
FINISHED BLOCK SIZE: 11" x 11" (28 cm x 28 cm)

CUTTING OUT THE PIECES

*Follow **Rotary Cutting**, page 50, to cut fabric. All strips are cut across the width of the fabric unless otherwise noted. Cutting lengths given for borders are exact. All measurements include a $1/4$" seam allowance.*

From pink solid:
- Cut 10 strips $6^3/4$"w. From these strips, cut 50 **squares** $6^3/4$" x $6^3/4$".
- Cut 2 *lengthwise* **top/bottom border strips** $3^1/2$" x $67^1/2$".
- Cut 2 *lengthwise* **side border strips** $3^1/2$" x 78".

From remaining width:
- Cut 3 strips $3^1/2$"w. From these strips, cut 16 **sashing squares** $3^1/2$" x $3^1/2$".

From white solid:
- Cut 10 strips $6^3/4$"w. From these strips, cut 50 **squares** $6^3/4$" x $6^3/4$".
- Cut 2 *lengthwise* **top/bottom border strips** $2^3/4$" x $67^1/2$".
- Cut 2 *lengthwise* **side border strips** $2^3/4$" x 78".

From remaining width:
- Cut 5 strips $11^1/2$"w. From these strips, cut 40 **sashing strips** $3^1/2$" x $11^1/2$".

YARDAGE REQUIREMENTS

Yardage is based on 43"/44" (109 cm/112 cm) wide fabric.

$5^3/8$ yds (4.9 m) of pink solid fabric (includes binding)

$4^1/2$ yds (4.1 m) of white solid fabric

$7^1/4$ yds (6.6 m) of backing fabric

You will also need: 86" x 86" (218 cm x 218 cm) square of batting

Fabric marking pen

"The decision to build a park in Virginia's mountains seemed to be moving forward at a rapid rate, despite all the reasons against it. Some mountain people had simply packed and gone, accepting the inevitable. The residents could no longer ignore the fact that their lives were about to change forever."

—from Lover's Knot

29

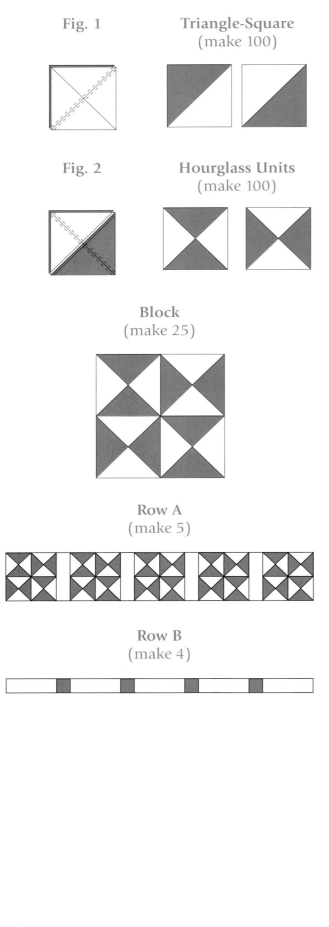

Fig. 1

Triangle-Square
(make 100)

Fig. 2

Hourglass Units
(make 100)

Block
(make 25)

Row A
(make 5)

Row B
(make 4)

ASSEMBLING THE QUILT TOP

*Follow **Piecing and Pressing**, page 51, to assemble the quilt top.*

1. Draw a diagonal line in both directions on wrong side of each white **square**. With right sides together, place 1 white **square** on top of 1 pink **square**. Stitch ¼" from each side of 1 drawn line (**Fig. 1**).

2. Cut along drawn line and press open to make 2 **Triangle-Squares**. Make 100 **Triangle-Squares**.

3. On wrong side of 50 Triangle-Squares, extend drawn line from corner of white print triangle to corner of pink print triangle.

4. Place 1 marked Triangle-Square on top of 1 unmarked Triangle-Square with white triangles opposite each other and marked unit on top. Stitch ¼" from each side of drawn line (**Fig. 2**). Cut apart along drawn line to make 2 **Hourglass Units**; press open. Make 100 **Hourglass Units**.

5. Sew 4 **Hourglass Units** together to make **Block**. Make 25 **Blocks**.

6. Sew 5 **Blocks** and 4 **sashing strips** together to make **Row A**. Make 5 **Row A's**.

7. Sew 5 **sashing strips** and 4 **sashing squares** together to make **Row B**. Make 4 **Row B's**.

8. Sew **Row A's** and **Row B's** together to complete **Quilt Top Center**.

ADDING THE BORDERS

1. Sew 1 **pink top/bottom border strip** and 1 **white top/bottom border strip** together lengthwise to make **top/bottom border**. Make 2 **top/bottom borders**.

2. Sew 1 **pink side border strip** and 1 **white side border strip** together lengthwise to make **side border**. Make 2 **side borders**.

3. Sew 1 **top/bottom border** to opposite sides of **Quilt Top Center**.

4. Sew 1 **side border** to remaining sides of **Quilt Top Center**.

5. Matching shiny sides, fold a piece of freezer paper in half. Place fold on dashed line of **Corner Scallop** pattern, page 33. Trace pattern; cut out.With shiny side down, place straight edge of pattern on seam between white and pink borders. Iron the corner scallop pattern to one corner of the Quilt Top. Trace around the scallop with fabric marking pen. Repeat for remaining corners of Quilt Top.

6. Trace **Scallop** pattern, page 33, onto dull side of freezer paper; cut out along traced line. With shiny side down and matching repeat arrows, place straight edge of pattern on seam between borders . Iron the pattern to the Quilt Top. Trace around the scallop with fabric marking pen. Repeat along 1 side of Quilt Top. Repeat for remaining sides of Quilt Top.

COMPLETING THE QUILT TOP

1. Follow **Quilting**, page 54, to mark, layer, and quilt as desired. Our quilt is hand quilted with channel quilting and large circles in the Hourglass Blocks, small circles in the sashings and scalloped echo quilting in the borders.

2. To prepare quilt for binding, Straight Stitch around quilt on drawn scallop line. Trim borders $1/8$" outside stitching line.

3. Cut a 28" square of binding fabric. Follow **Making Continuous Bias Binding**, page 60, to make approximately 9 yds of 2"w bias binding. Press one end of binding diagonally.

4. Beginning with pressed end and matching raw edges of binding to raw edge of quilt top, pin binding to front of quilt, easing binding around curved edges. Sew binding to quilt until binding overlaps beginning end by approximately 1". Trim excess binding. Fold binding over to quilt backing and pin in place, covering stitching line. Blindstitch, page 63, binding to backing.

Quilt Top Diagram

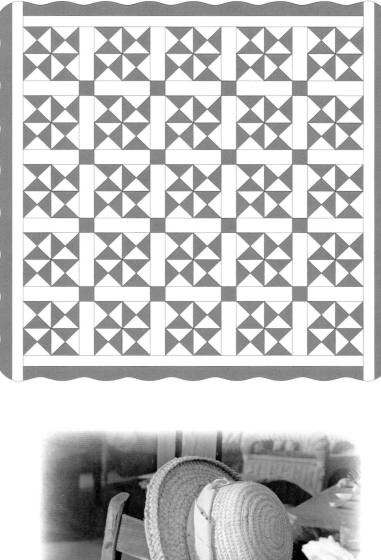

"*Kendra picked up the small pile of quilts and set them next to Helen. Then she perched on the sofa beside them and unfolded the top one, a simple two-color pattern of bright pink and white. 'Look how small these stitches are.'*

'Yes indeed,' Helen said. 'That's Big Dipper, by the way. My mama and her friends made one like this when our preacher moved away.'"

—from Lover's Knot

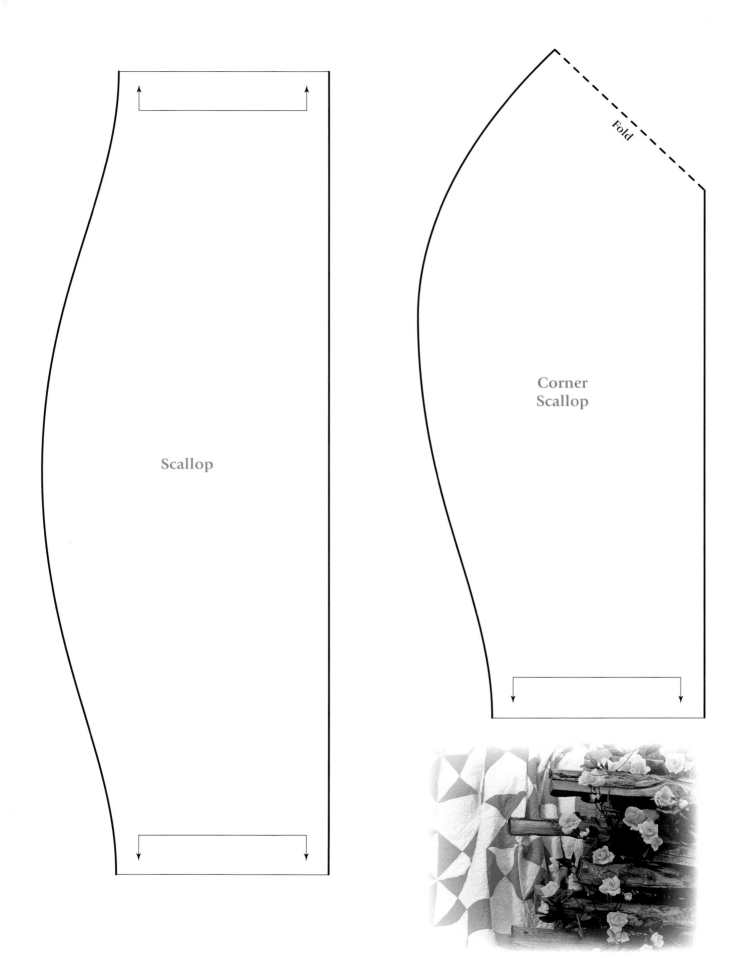

Scallop

Corner
Scallop

Fold

Churn Dash Quilt

The Churn Dash block is a venerable favorite among quilters. Our quilt gets its fresh appeal from the simplicity of its two-fabric design scheme. In the early 1900s, having a large amount of any single fabric with which to quilt would have been a rare luxury, so Kendra's quilt could easily have been "scrappy" with lots of fabrics.

FINISHED QUILT SIZE: 74" x 85" (188 cm x 216 cm)
FINISHED BLOCK SIZE: 11" x 11" (28 cm x 28 cm)

CUTTING OUT THE PIECES

*Follow **Rotary Cutting**, page 50, to cut fabric. All measurements include a ¹/₄" seam allowance.*

From green solid:
- Cut 10 strips 4¹/₈"w. From these strips, cut 84 **small squares** 4¹/₈" x 4¹/₈".
- Cut 2 *lengthwise* **top/bottom border strips** 2" x 82".
- Cut 2 *lengthwise* **side border strips** 2" x 91".

From remaining width:
- Cut 12 strips 5"w. From these strips, cut 168 **rectangles** 2¹/₈" x 5".

From white solid:
- Cut 10 strips 4¹/₈"w. From these strips, cut 84 **small squares** 4¹/₈" x 4¹/₈".
- Cut 9 **binding strips** 2¹/₂"w.
- Cut 2 *lengthwise* **top/bottom border strips** 2¹/₂" x 82".
- Cut 2 *lengthwise* **side border strips** 2¹/₂" x 91".

From remaining width:
- Cut 12 strips 5"w. From these strips, cut 168 **rectangles** 2¹/₈" x 5".
- Cut 7 strips 5"w. From these strips, cut 42 **large squares** 5" x 5".

YARDAGE REQUIREMENTS

Yardage is based on 43"/44" (109 cm/112 cm) wide fabric.

4¹/₈ yds (3.8 m) of green solid fabric

4⁷/₈ yds (4.5 m) of white solid fabric (includes binding)

6⁷/₈ yds (6.3 m) of backing fabric

You will also need: 82" x 93" (208 cm x 236 cm) rectangle of batting

"What her sister liked best, Leah knew, was cooking meals, baking whatever the cupboard allowed, sewing clothes and making quilts."
—from Lover's Knot

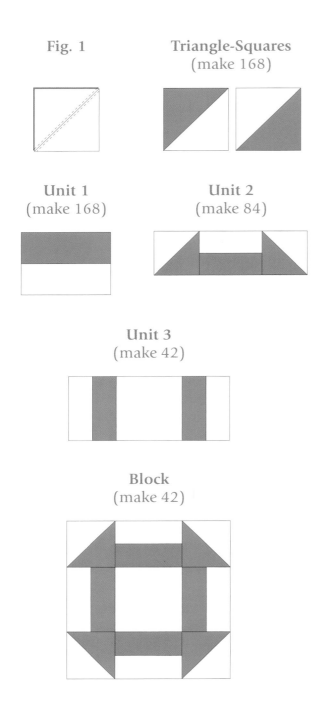

Fig. 1

Triangle-Squares
(make 168)

Unit 1
(make 168)

Unit 2
(make 84)

Unit 3
(make 42)

Block
(make 42)

ASSEMBLING THE QUILT TOP

*Follow **Piecing and Pressing**, page 51, to assemble the quilt top.*

1. Draw a diagonal line on wrong side of each white solid **small square**. With right sides together, place 1 white solid **small square** on top of 1 green solid **small square**. Stitch seam $1/4$" from each side of drawn line (**Fig. 1**).

2. Cut along drawn line and press seam allowances to darker fabric to make 2 **Triangle-Squares**. Make 168 **Triangle-Squares**.

3. Sew 1 white solid **rectangle** and 1 green solid **rectangle** together lengthwise to make **Unit 1**. Make 168 **Unit 1's**.

4. Sew 2 **Triangle-Squares** and 1 **Unit 1** together to make **Unit 2**. Make 84 **Unit 2's**.

5. Sew 2 **Unit 1's** and 1 **large square** together to make **Unit 3**. Make 42 **Unit 3's**.

6. Sew 2 **Unit 2's** and 1 **Unit 3** together to make **Block**. Make 42 **Blocks**.

7. Sew 6 **Blocks** together to make a **Row**. Make 7 **Rows**.

8. Sew **Rows** together to complete **Quilt Top Center**.

"'You think the government can pay enough for what this holler means to us? My family's been here for nigh two hundred years. And yours nearly as long. These mountains belong to us. We bought what we own with the blood of the people who went before us.'"
—Jesse Spurlock

ADDING THE BORDERS

1. Sew 1 white solid **top border strip** and 1 green solid **top border strip** together lengthwise to make **Top Border**. Mark center of 1 long edge of Top Border.

2. Measure across center of Quilt Top. Mark the center of each edge of Quilt Top (**Fig. 2**). Matching center marks and raw edges, pin border to Quilt Top edge. Beginning at center mark of border, measure ¹/₂ the width of the Quilt Top in both directions and mark border. Match marks on border with corners of quilt top and pin. Easing in any fullness, pin border to Quilt Top. Sew border to Quilt Top, beginning and ending seam exactly ¹/₄" from each corner of Quilt Top and backstitching at beginning and end of stitching (**Fig. 3**).

3. Repeat **Steps** 2 and 3 to sew bottom, then side borders to Quilt Top. To keep top and bottom borders out of the way when attaching side borders, fold and pin as shown in **Fig. 4**.

4. Fold 1 corner of Quilt Top diagonally with right sides together and matching edges. Use ruler to mark stitching line as shown in **Fig. 5**. Pin borders together along drawn line. Sew on drawn line, backstitching at beginning and end of stitching (**Fig. 6**)

5. Turn mitered corner right side up. Check to make sure corner will lie flat with no gaps or puckers.

6. Trim seam allowances to ¹/₄"; press to one side.

7. Repeat **Steps** 4-6 to miter each remaining corner.

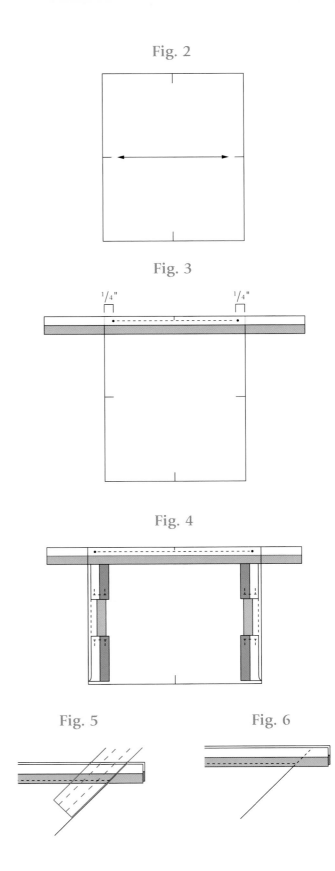

Fig. 2

Fig. 3

Fig. 4

Fig. 5

Fig. 6

COMPLETING THE QUILT TOP

1. Follow **Quilting,** page 54, to mark, layer, and quilt as desired. Our quilt is hand quilted with outline quilting in all the green rectangles and triangles. There is a flower motif in the center of each Churn Dash Block and 4 wavy lines of echo quilting in the borders.

2. Use binding strips and follow **Making Straight-Grain Binding,** page 61, to prepare binding.

3. Follow **Attaching Binding With Mitered Corners**, page 61, to bind quilt.

Quilt Top Diagram

"This Churn Dash was a fund raiser, I'll just bet you. Some church or school made a little money from this one."

—Helen Henry

Log Cabin Quilt

There's no doubt about it, this is Kendra's cozy Log Cabin quilt—minus the signatures, of course. This lap throw was quilted with wavy lines where the light and dark meet on each block. It's an excellent technique to soften the contrast between hue and shade. It's also fun, because when you aren't trying to quilt in straight lines, you can just relax and let the quilting happen.

FINISHED QUILT SIZE: 55" x 67" (140 cm x 170 cm)
FINISHED BLOCK SIZE: 12" x 12" (30 cm x 30 cm)

CUTTING OUT THE PIECES

*Follow **Rotary Cutting**, page 50, to cut fabric. All measurements include a 1/4" seam allowance.*

From gold solid:
- Cut 2 strips 3½"w. From these strips, cut 20 **squares (A)** 3½" x 3½".

From assorted light tan prints:
- Cut 20 **rectangles (B)** 2" x 3½".
- Cut 20 **rectangles (C)** 2" x 5".

From assorted rust prints:
- Cut 20 **rectangles (F)** 2" x 6½".
- Cut 20 **rectangles (G)** 2" x 8".

From assorted dark tan prints:
- Cut 20 **rectangles (J)** 2" x 9½".
- Cut 20 **rectangles (K)** 2" x 11".

From light brown prints:
- Cut 20 **rectangles (D)** 2" x 5".
- Cut 20 **rectangles (E)** 2" x 6½".

From assorted medium brown prints:
- Cut 20 **rectangles (H)** 2" x 8".
- Cut 20 **rectangles (I)** 2" x 9½".

From assorted dark brown prints:
- Cut 20 **rectangles (L)** 2" x 11".
- Cut 20 **rectangles (M)** 2" x 12½".

From dark brown fabric:
- Cut 6 **border strips** 3½" wide.

YARDAGE REQUIREMENTS

Yardage is based on 43"/44" (109 cm/112 cm) wide fabric.

1/4 yd (23 cm) of gold solid fabric

3/8 yd (34 cm) **total** of assorted light tan print fabrics

1/2 yd (46 cm) **total** of assorted rust print fabrics

3/4 yd (69 cm) **total** of assorted dark tan print fabrics

3/8 yd (34 cm) **total** of assorted light brown print fabrics

5/8 yd (57 cm) **total** of assorted medium brown print fabrics

3/4 yd (69 cm) **total** of assorted dark brown print fabrics

1½ yds (1.4 m) of dark brown fabric (includes binding)

4¼ yds (3.9 m) of backing fabric

You will also need:
63" x 75" (160 cm x 191 cm) rectangle of batting

"Helen arrived about three carrying a discount store shopping bag. On the porch she thrust it in Kendra's direction with complete lack of ceremony. 'Something for you. Call it a housewarming present.'

Kendra pulled a quilt from the bag and shook it out. It was a Log Cabin in scrappy earth tones, browns, beiges, grays, and olive. The large center squares were a sunny gold, and the light and dark halves of each block had been laid out to resemble furrows. Best of all, names were penned in the center squares. Kendra recognized the names of the SCC quilters she'd met.

She cleared her throat, which felt as if it was suddenly stuffed with quilt batting. 'I don't know what to say. It's just so beautiful. And perfect.'

'Log Cabin seemed appropriate, considering this useless pile of timber you're calling home now. And we knew you liked friendship quilts.'"

—from Lover's Knot

Unit 1

Unit 2

Unit 3

Unit 4

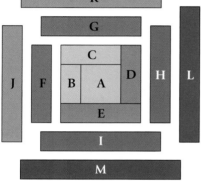

Block Assembly Diagram

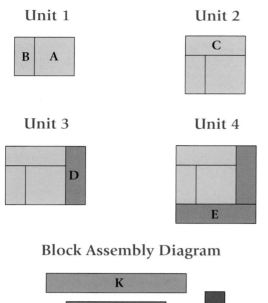

Block
(make 20)

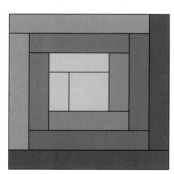

ASSEMBLING THE QUILT TOP

Follow Piecing and Pressing, page 51, to assemble the quilt top.

1. Sew **square** (A) and **rectangle** (B) together to make **Unit 1**.

2. Sew **rectangle** (C) to top edge of Unit 1 to make **Unit 2**.

3. Sew **rectangle** (D) to right edge of Unit 2 to make **Unit 3**.

4. Sew **rectangle** (E) to bottom edge of Unit 3 to make **Unit 4**.

5. Following **Block Assembly Diagram**, continue sewing **rectangles** to Unit 4, working clockwise and in alphabetical order as shown to make **Block**. Make 20 **Blocks**.

6. Refering to **photo** and rotating blocks as shown, sew 4 **Blocks** together to make **Row**. Make 5 **Rows**.

7. Sew Rows together to make **Quilt Top Center**.

ADDING THE BORDERS

1. Sew **border strips** together end to end to make 1 continuous border strip.

2. To determine length of side borders, measure *length* across center of Quilt Top Center. Cut 2 **side borders** the determined length. Matching centers and corners, sew **side borders** to Quilt Top Center.

3. To determine length of top/bottom borders, measure *width* across center of Quilt Top Center (including added borders). Cut 2 **top/bottom borders** the determined length. Matching centers and corners, sew **top/bottom borders** to Quilt Top Center.

COMPLETING THE QUILT TOP

1. Follow **Quilting,** page 54, to mark, layer, and quilt as desired. Our quilt is machine quilted with a wavy line between each dark rectangle and a feather design running diagonally through the light-colored areas.

2. Cut a 26" square of binding fabric. Follow **Making Continuous Bias Binding**, page 60, to make $7^{1}/_{8}$ yds of $2^{1}/_{4}$"w binding.

3. Follow **Attaching Binding With Mitered Corners**, page 61, to bind quilt.

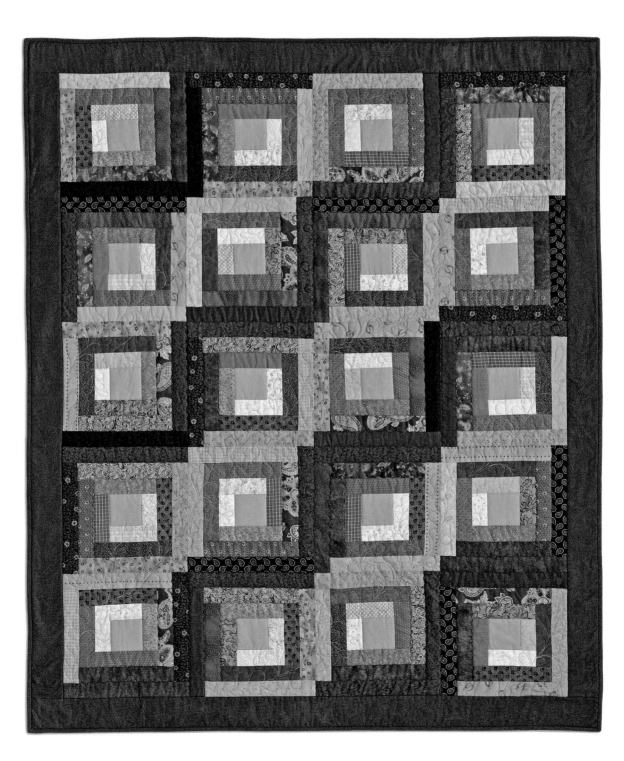

Cactus Bloom Quilt

Here's your chance to experiment with color! A cactus can bloom in almost any hue, so be sure and use your favorite fabrics to create your desert garden. The SCC Bee, or Shenandoah Community Church quilters, chose this pattern for their fundraising quilt because it symbolized their hope for success with their outreach ministry.

FINISHED QUILT SIZE 47" x 47" (119 cm x 119 cm)
FINISHED BLOCK SIZE: 12" x 12" (30 cm x 30 cm)

CUTTING OUT THE PIECES

*Follow **Rotary Cutting**, page 50, to cut fabric. Borders include an extra 4" of length for "insurance" and will be trimmed after assembling quilt top center. All other measurements include a $^1/_4$" seam allowance. Refer to **Template Cutting**, page 50, to use templates, page 49.*

From gold print:
- Cut 6 **background squares** $14^1/_2$" x $14^1/_2$".
- Cut 2 *lengthwise* **outer side borders** $4^1/_2$" x $42^1/_2$".
- Cut 2 *lengthwise* **outer top/bottom borders** $4^1/_2$" x $50^1/_2$".

From remaining width cut:
- Cut 3 **background squares** $14^1/_2$" x $14^1/_2$".

From green print:
- Cut 9 **circles** using template A.
- Cut 72 **leaves** using template B.

From red print:
- Cut 2 *lengthwise* **side inner borders** $1^1/_2$" x $40^1/_2$".
- Cut 2 *lengthwise* **top/bottom inner borders** $1^1/_2$" x $42^1/_2$".

From remaining width cut:
- Cut 9 **blossoms** using template C.

"*It was just past eight when Kendra knocked on Helen's door. Helen greeted her, saying, 'I've just been finishing the binding on a quilt for the church fair next weekend.'*

The fair was a fundraiser for the church's outreach ministry to prisoners. 'What kind of quilt,' Kendra asked.

'It's an old pattern my Aunt Mavis made once upon a time, called Cactus Bloom. I still have her templates, cut from Cream of Wheat boxes after she traced the pattern from some newspaper or booklet. We thought maybe it was a good one for this. Even a prickly cactus can flower if it's given the chance.'"

—from Lover's Knot

YARDAGE REQUIREMENTS

Yardage is based on 43"/44" (109 cm/112 cm) wide fabric.

$3^5/_8$ yds (3.3 m) of gold print fabric (includes binding)

$^5/_8$ yd (57 cm) of green print fabric

$1^3/_8$ yds (1.3 m) of red print fabric

$3^1/_8$ yds (2.9 m) of backing fabric

You will also need:
55" x 55" (140 cm x 140 cm) square of batting

No-melt mylar template plastic

Spray starch

Paintbrush

Block (make 9)

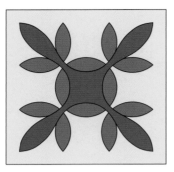

ASSEMBLING THE QUILT TOP
Follow **Piecing and Pressing**, *page 51, and* **Mock Hand Appliqué**, *page 52, to make the blocks.*

1. Center 1 **circle** on 1 gold **background square** and appliqué in place. Center 1 **blossom** over circle and appliqué in place. Place 8 **leaves** near ends of blossom and appliqué in place. Making sure appliquéd design is centered, trim **background square** to $12^1/2$" x $12^1/2$" to make **Block**. Make 9 **Blocks**.

2. Sew 3 **Blocks** together to make **Row**. Make 3 **Rows**.

3. Sew Rows together to complete **Quilt Top Center**.

ADDING THE BORDERS
Refer to **Quilt Top Diagram** *for placement.*

1. To determine length of **side inner borders**, measure *length* across center of Quilt Top Center. Cut 2 **side inner borders** the determined length. Matching centers and corners, sew **side inner borders** to Quilt Top Center.

2. To determine length of **top/bottom inner borders**, measure *width* across center of Quilt Top Center (including added borders). Trim **top/bottom inner borders** to determined length. Matching centers and corners, sew **top/bottom inner borders** to Quilt Top Center.

3. Repeat **Steps 1–2** to sew **outer borders** to Quilt Top.

"'You buy your quilt raffle tickets yet,' Helen asked. Kendra had only seen the Cactus Bloom quilt from a distance, but she was satisfied it was a stunner. 'I'll buy a bunch. I promise.'"

—from Lover's Knot

COMPLETING THE QUILT

1. Follow **Quilting,** page 54, to mark, layer, and quilt as desired. Our quilt is machine quilted with a wavy feather design in the borders. There is free-motion quilting consisting of closely-spaced lines and shapes, commonly referred to as "McTavishing," in the block backgrounds.

2. Cut a 23" square of binding fabric. Follow **Making Continuous Bias Binding,** page 60, to make $5^5/_8$ yds of $2^1/_4$"w binding.

3. Follow **Attaching Binding With Mitered Corners**, page 61, to bind quilt.

Quilt Top Diagram

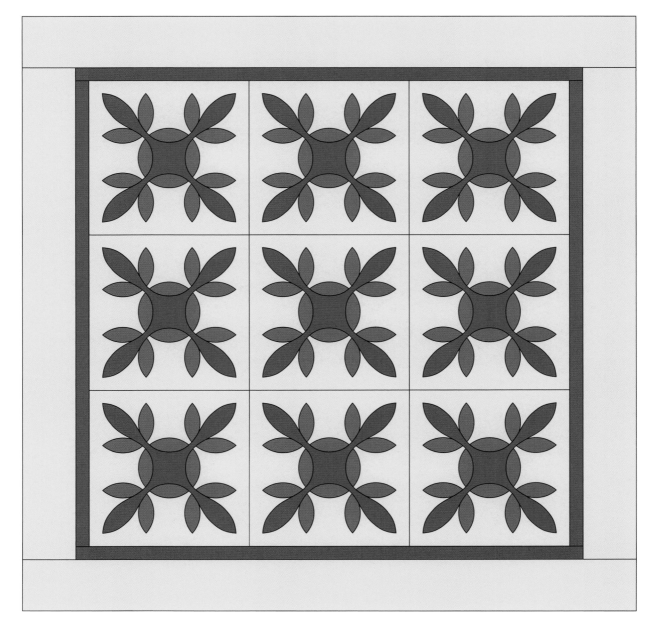

"'You got imagination, I can see that for sure. A good thing in a quilter.'"
—Helen Henry to Kendra Taylor

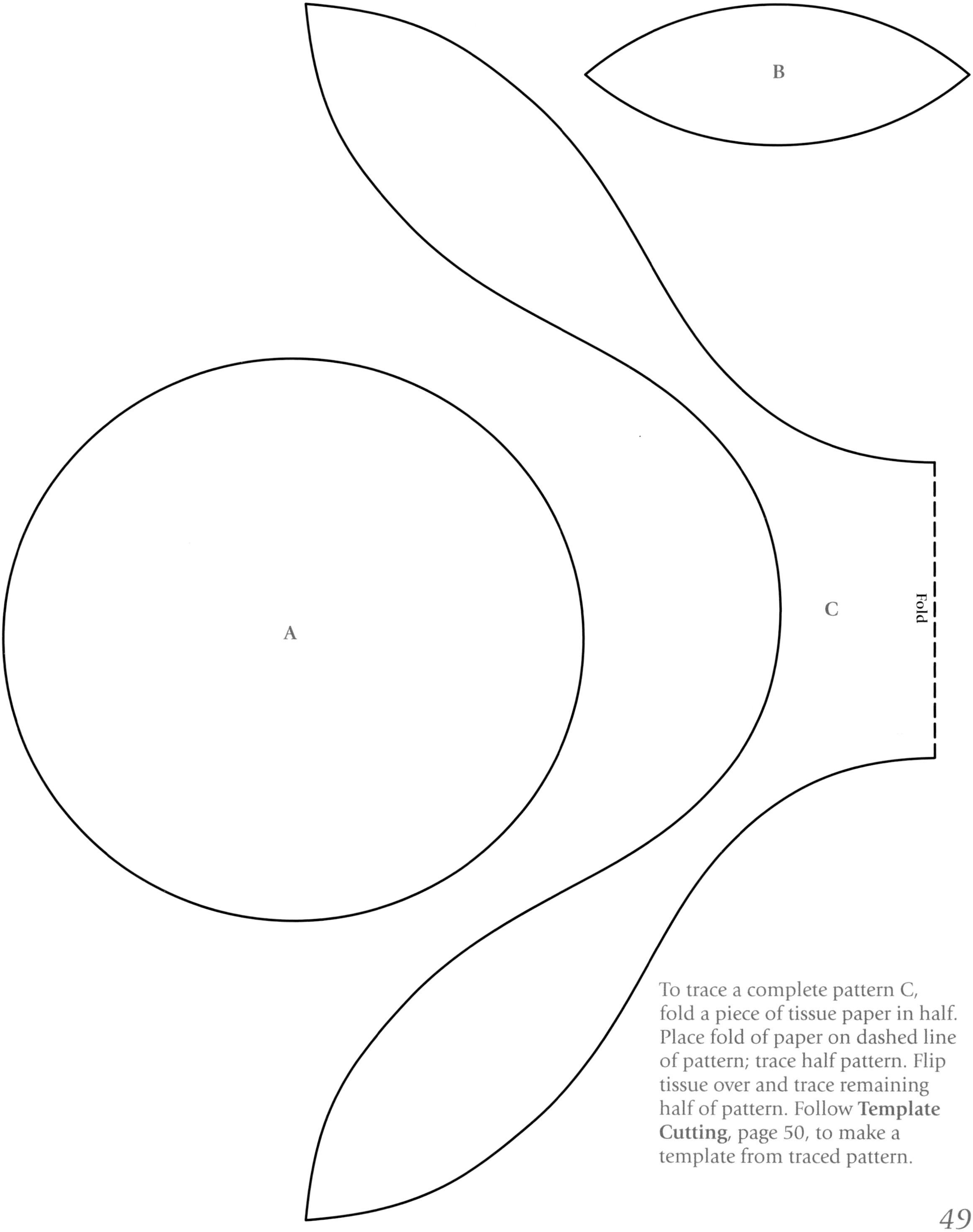

B

A

C

Fold

To trace a complete pattern C, fold a piece of tissue paper in half. Place fold of paper on dashed line of pattern; trace half pattern. Flip tissue over and trace remaining half of pattern. Follow **Template Cutting**, page 50, to make a template from traced pattern.

General Instructions

Complete instructions are given for making each of the projects shown in this book. To make your project easier and more enjoyable, we encourage you to carefully read all the general instructions, study the color photographs, and familiarize yourself with the individual project instructions before beginning a project.

Fig. 1

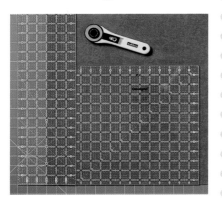

Fig. 2

Fig. 3

ROTARY CUTTING

Rotary cutting has brought speed and accuracy to quiltmaking by allowing quilters to easily cut strips of fabric and then cut those strips into smaller pieces.

- Place fabric on work surface with fold closest to you.

- Cut all strips from the selvage-to-selvage width of the fabric unless otherwise indicated in project instructions.

- Square left edge of fabric using rotary cutter and rulers (**Figs. 1 - 2**).

- To cut each strip required for a project, place the ruler over the cut edge of the fabric, aligning desired marking on the ruler with the cut edge (**Fig. 3**); make the cut.

- When cutting several strips from a single piece of fabric, it is important to make sure that cuts remain at a perfect right angle to the fold; square fabric as needed.

TEMPLATE CUTTING

Our piecing template patterns include a ¹/₄" seam allowance. Patterns for appliqué templates do not include seam allowances. .

1. To make a template from a pattern, use a permanent fine-point pen to carefully trace the pattern onto template plastic, making sure to transfer all markings. Cut out template along outer drawn line. Check template against original pattern for accuracy.
2. To use a piecing template, place template on wrong side of fabric, aligning grain line on template with straight grain of fabric. Use a sharp fabric marking pencil to draw around template. Cut out fabric piece using scissors or rotary cutting equipment.
3. To use an appliqué template, place template on wrong side of appliqué fabric for Mock Hand Appliqué or right side for Needle-Turn Appliqué . Use a pencil to lightly draw around template, leaving at least ¹/₂" between shapes; repeat for number of appliqués specified in project instructions. Cut out shapes a scant ¹/₄" outside drawn line.

PIECING AND PRESSING

Precise cutting, followed by accurate piecing and careful pressing, will ensure that all the pieces of your quilt top fit together well.

PIECING

- Set sewing machine stitch length for approximately 11 stitches per inch.

- Use a neutral-colored general-purpose sewing thread (not quilting thread) in the needle and in the bobbin.

- An accurate $1/4$" seam allowance is ***essential***. Presser feet that are $1/4$" wide are available for most sewing machines.

- When piecing, always place pieces ***right sides*** together and match raw edges; pin if necessary.

- Chain piecing saves time and will usually result in more accurate piecing.

- Trim away points of seam allowances that extend beyond edges of sewn seams.

Sewing Across Seam Intersections

When sewing across the intersection of two seams, place pieces right sides together and match seams exactly, making sure seam allowances are pressed in opposite directions (**Fig. 4**).

Sewing Strip Sets

When there are several strips to assemble into a strip set, first sew the strips together into pairs, then sew the pairs together to form the strip set. To help avoid distortion, sew 1 seam in 1 direction and then sew the next seam in the opposite direction (**Fig. 5**).

Fig. 4

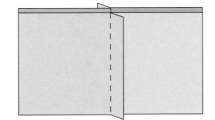

Fig. 5

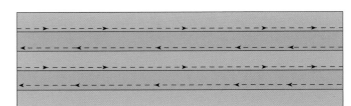

PRESSING

- Use a steam iron set on "Cotton" for all pressing.

- Press after sewing each seam

- Seam allowances are almost always pressed to one side, usually toward the darker fabric. However, to reduce bulk it may occasionally be necessary to press seam allowances toward the lighter fabric or even to press them open.

- To prevent a dark fabric seam allowance from showing through a light fabric, trim the darker seam allowance slightly narrower than the lighter seam allowance.

- To press long seams, such as those in long strip sets, without curving or other distortion, lay strips across the width of the ironing board.

APPLIQUÉ
NEEDLE-TURN APPLIQUÉ

*In this traditional hand appliqué method, the needle is used to turn the seam allowance under as you sew the appliqué to the background fabric using a Blind Stitch, page 63 (**Fig. 42**). Stitches on the right side of fabric should not show. Stitches on the edge of an appliqué and on background fabric should be equal in length. It is not necessary to appliqué areas that will be enclosed in a seam.*

1. Thread a sharps needle with a single strand of general-purpose sewing thread the color of the appliqué; knot one end.
2. Begin on as straight an edge as possible and use point of needle to turn under a small amount of seam allowance, concealing drawn line on appliqué. Blindstitch appliqué to the background, turning under the seam allowance and stitching to completely secure appliqué.

MOCK HAND APPLIQUÉ

This technique uses a machine zigzag stitch to achieve a look that closely resembles traditional hand appliqué. Appliqués are prepared by pressing the fabric edges over the template edges. The appliqués are then stitched to the background square.

1. Clip inner curves of appliqué shape; do not clip outer curves or outward points (**Fig. 6**). Take care to clip close to, but not through drawn line. Clipped areas should be secured with a few extra stitches when appliquéing to reduce stress and prevent fraying.
2. Cover a section of ironing board with a piece of scrap fabric. Set iron on cotton setting (without steam).

> *"Helen Henry? Now there's a character. She'll get you quilting. See if she don't.'"*
> —Cash Rosslyn to
> Kendra Taylor

Fig. 6

3. Place appliqué wrong side up on ironing board.
4. Center template on appliqué. Spray a small amount of starch into the cap of the can to make liquid starch. Dip paintbrush into starch. Beginning on as straight an edge as possible, brush starch on 2-3" of seam allowance.
5. Fold a small amount of starched seam allowance over template. Being sure template does not move, carefully press seam allowance.
6. When you are approximately ³/₄" from an outward point, fold seam allowance over template at point as shown in **Fig. 7** and press.
7. Fold seam allowance over template on one side of point and press (**Fig. 8**).
8. Fold seam allowance over template on opposite side of point and press (**Fig. 9**). (*Note: On narrow outward points, seam allowance may extend beyond template. Carefully trim excess seam allowance to just inside edge of template.*)
9. Continue applying starch and pressing seam allowance. Remove template and press again.
10. Trim seam allowance to approximately ³/₁₆".
11. Thread sewing machine with transparent monofilament thread; use general-purpose thread that matches background fabric in bobbin.
12. Set sewing machine for a narrow zigzag stitch (just wide enough to catch 2 or 3 threads of the appliqué) and a short to medium stitch length.
13. Arrange appliqué on background square as described in project instructions. Use pins or hand baste to secure.
14. Sew around edges of each appliqué so that the zigzag stitches barely catch the folded edge of the appliqué (**Fig. 10**).
15. It is not necessary to backstitch at beginning or end of stitching. End stitching by sewing ¹/₄" over the first stitches. Trim thread ends close to fabric.

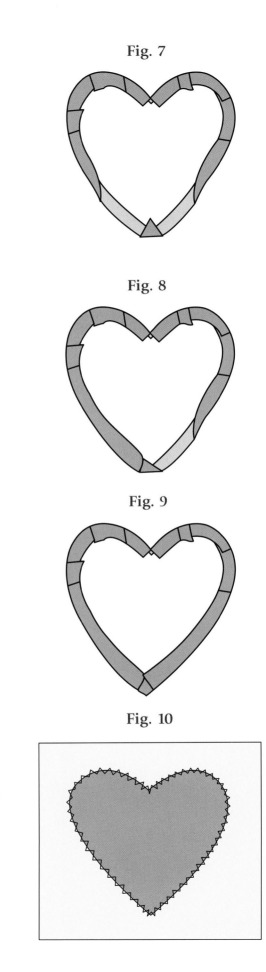

Fig. 7

Fig. 8

Fig. 9

Fig. 10

Fig. 11

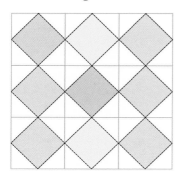

Fig. 12

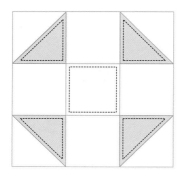

Fig. 13

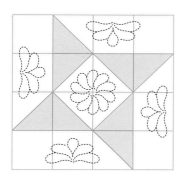

Fig. 14

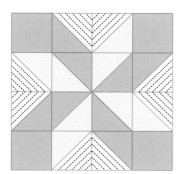

QUILTING

Quilting holds the 3 layers (top, batting, and backing) of the quilt together and can be done by hand or machine. Because marking, layering, and quilting are interrelated and may be done in different orders depending on circumstances, please read the entire **Quilting** *section, pages 54 - 59, before beginning project.*

TYPES OF QUILTING
In the Ditch Quilting

Quilting along seamlines or along edges of appliquéd pieces is called "in the ditch" quilting (**Fig. 11**). This type of quilting should be done on the side **opposite** the seam allowance and does not need to be marked.

Outline Quilting

Quilting a consistent distance, usually $1/4$", from a seam or appliqué is called "outline" quilting (**Fig. 12**). Outline quilting may be marked, or $1/4$"w masking tape may be placed along seamlines for a quilting guide. (Do not leave tape on quilt longer than necessary, since it may leave an adhesive residue.)

Motif Quilting

Quilting a design, such as a feathered wreath is called "motif" quilting (**Fig. 13**). This type of quilting should be marked before basting quilt layers together.

Echo Quilting

Quilting that follows the outline of an appliquéd or pieced design with 2 or more parallel lines is called "echo" quilting (**Fig.14**). This type of quilting does not need to be marked.

"I guess that's part of the reason Isaac's quilt intrigues me. It must have meant so much to Leah. She left it for Isaac, even though she had no idea where he was or if a quilt was something he'd care about.'"

—Kendra Taylor

Channel Quilting

Quilting with straight, parallel lines is called "channel" quilting (**Fig. 15**). This type of quilting may be marked or stitched using a guide.

Crosshatch Quilting

Quilting straight lines in a grid pattern is called "crosshatch" quilting (**Fig.16**). Lines may be stitched parallel to edges of quilt or stitched diagonally. This type of quilting may be marked or stitched using a guide.

Stipple Quilting

Meandering quilting that is very closely spaced is called "stipple" quilting (**Fig.17**). Stippling will flatten the area quilted and is often stitched in background areas to raise appliquéd or pieced designs. This type of quilting does not need to be marked.

MARKING QUILTING LINES

Quilting lines may be marked using fabric marking pencils, chalk markers, water-or air-soluble pens, or lead pencils.

Simple quilting designs may be marked with chalk or chalk pencil after basting. A small area may be marked, then quilted, before moving to next area to be marked. Intricate designs should be marked before basting using a more durable marker.

Caution: Pressing may permanently set some marks. Test different markers **on scrap fabric** to find one that marks clearly and can be thoroughly removed.

A wide variety of precut quilting stencils, as well as entire books of quilting patterns, are available. Using a stencil makes it easier to mark intricate or repetitive designs on your quilt top.

To make a stencil from a pattern, center template plastic over pattern and use a permanent marker to trace pattern onto plastic. Use a craft knife with a single or double blade to cut narrow slits along traced lines (**Fig. 18**). Use desired marking tool and stencil to mark quilting lines.

Fig. 15

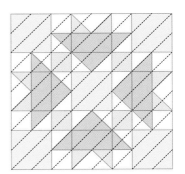

Fig. 16

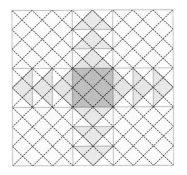

Fig. 17

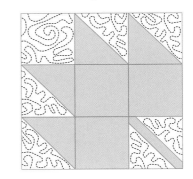

Fig. 18

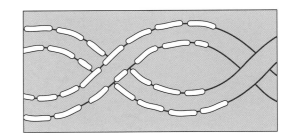

55

PREPARING THE BACKING

To allow for slight shifting of quilt top during quilting, backing should be approximately 4" larger on all sides. Yardage requirements listed for quilt backings are calculated for 43"/44"w fabric. Using 90"w or 108"w fabric for the backing of a bed-sized quilt may eliminate piecing. To piece a backing using 43"/44"w fabric, use the following instructions.

Fig. 19

1. Measure length and width of quilt top; add 8" to each measurement.
2. If determined width is 79" or less, cut backing fabric into two lengths slightly longer than determined **length** measurement. Trim selvages. Place lengths with right sides facing and sew long edges together, forming tube (**Fig. 19**). Match seams and press along one fold (**Fig. 20**). Cut along pressed fold to form single piece (**Fig. 21**).
3. If determined width is more than 79", it may require less fabric yardage if the backing is pieced horizontally. Divide determined **length** measurement by 40" to determine how many widths will be needed. Cut required number of widths the determined **width** measurement. Trim selvages. Sew long edges together to form single piece.
4. Trim backing to size determined in Step 1; press seam allowances open.

Fig. 20

CHOOSING AND PREPARING THE BATTING

Choosing the right batting will make your quilting job easier. The projects in this book are made using cotton batting which does not require tight quilting. If machine quilting, choose a low-loft all cotton or a cotton/polyester blend batting because the cotton helps "grip" the layers of the quilt. For hand quilting, choose a low-loft batting in any of the fiber types described here.

Fig. 21

Batting options include cotton/polyester batting, which combines the best of both polyester and cotton battings; fusible battings which do not need to be basted before quilting; bonded polyester which is treated with a protective coating to stabilize the fibers and to reduce "bearding," a process in which batting fibers work their way out through the quilt fabrics; and wool and silk battings, which are generally more expensive and usually only dry-cleanable.

Whichever batting you choose, read the manufacturer's instructions closely for any special notes on care or preparation. When you're ready to use your chosen batting in a project, cut batting the same size as the prepared backing.

ASSEMBLING THE QUILT

1. Examine wrong side of quilt top closely; trim any seam allowances and clip any threads that may show through the front of the quilt. Press quilt top.
2. If quilt top is to be marked before layering, mark quilting lines (see **Marking Quilting Lines**, page 55).
3. Place backing wrong side up on a flat surface. Use masking tape to tape edges of backing to surface. Place batting on top of backing fabric. Smooth batting gently, being careful not to stretch or tear. Center quilt top right side up on batting.
4. If hand quilting, begin in the center and work toward the outer edges to hand baste all layers together. Use long stitches and place basting lines approximately 4" apart (**Fig. 22**). Smooth fullness or wrinkles toward outer edges.
5. If machine quilting, use 1" rustproof safety pins to "pin-baste" all layers together, spacing pins approximately 4" apart. Begin at the center and work toward the outer edges to secure all layers. If possible, place pins away from areas that will be quilted, although pins may be removed as needed when quilting.

Fig. 22

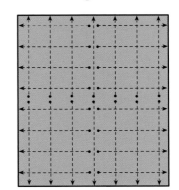

HAND QUILTING

The quilting stitch is a basic running stitch that forms a broken line on the quilt top and backing. Stitches on the quilt top and backing should be straight and equal in length.

1. Secure center of quilt in hoop or frame. Check quilt top and backing to make sure they are smooth. To help prevent puckers, always begin quilting in the center of the quilt and work toward the outside edges.
2. Thread needle with an 18"-20" length of quilting thread; knot 1 end. Using a thimble, insert needle into quilt top and batting approximately $1/2$" from where you wish to begin quilting. Bring needle up at the point where you wish to begin (**Fig. 23**); when knot catches on quilt top, give thread a quick, short pull to "pop" knot through fabric into batting (**Fig. 24**).
3. Holding the needle with your sewing hand and placing your other hand underneath the quilt, use thimble to push the tip of the needle down through all layers. As soon as needle touches your finger underneath, use that finger to push the tip of the needle only back up through the layers to top of quilt. (The amount of the needle showing above the fabric determines the length of the quilting stitch.) Referring to **Fig. 25**, rock the needle up and down, taking 3 - 6 stitches before bringing the needle and thread completely through the layers. Check the back of the quilt to make sure stitches are going through all layers. When quilting through a seam allowance or quilting a curve or corner, you may need to make 1 stitch at a time.

Fig. 23

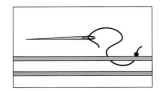

Fig. 24

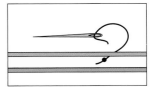

Fig. 25

"About tomorrow, let's go camping. I brought everything we'll need. I thought maybe we could go up to the park. Get off the beaten path a little and see what's up there. Maybe find Lock Hollow.'"

— Isaac Taylor to
Kendra Taylor

4. When you reach the end of your thread, knot thread close to the fabric and "pop" knot into batting; clip thread close to fabric.

5. Stop and move your hoop as often as necessary. You do not have to tie a knot every time you move your hoop; you may leave the thread dangling and pick it up again when you return to that part of the quilt.

STRAIGHT-LINE MACHINE QUILTING

The following instructions are for straight-line quilting, which requires a walking foot or even-feed foot. The term "straight-line" is somewhat deceptive, since curves (especially gentle ones) as well as straight lines can be stitched with this technique.

1. Using the same color general-purpose thread in the needle and bobbin avoids "dots" of bobbin thread being pulled to the surface.

2. Using general-purpose thread, which matches the backing, in the bobbin, will add pattern and dimension to the quilt back without adding contrasting color. Refer to your owner's manual for recommended tension settings.

3. Set the stitch length for 6 – 10 stitches per inch and attach the walking foot to sewing machine.

4. After pin-basting, decide which section of the quilt will have the longest continuous quilting line, oftentimes the area from center top to center bottom. Leaving the area exposed where you will place your first line of quilting, roll up each edge of the quilt to help reduce the bulk, keeping fabrics smooth. Smaller projects may not need to be rolled.

5. Start stitching at beginning of longest quilting line, using very short stitches for the first ¹/₄" to "lock" beginning of quilting line. Stitch across project, using one hand on each side of the walking foot to slightly spread the fabric and to guide the fabric through the machine. Lock stitches at end of quilting line.

6. Continue machine quilting, stitching longer quilting lines first to stabilize the quilt before moving on to other areas.

FREE-MOTION MACHINE QUILTING

Free-motion quilting may be free form or may follow a marked quilting pattern.

1. Using the same color general-purpose thread in the needle and bobbin avoids "dots" of bobbin thread being pulled to the surface. Use general-purpose thread in the bobbin and decorative thread for stitching, such as metallic, variegated or contrasting-colored general-purpose thread, when you desire the quilting to be more pronounced.
2. Use a darning foot and drop or cover feed dogs. Pull up bobbin thread and hold both thread ends while you stitch 2 or 3 stitches in place to lock thread. Cut threads near quilt surface.
3. Place hands lightly on quilt on either side of darning foot to slightly spread fabric and to move fabric through the machine. Even stitch length is achieved by using smooth, flowing hand motion and steady machine speed. Slow machine speed and fast hand movement will create long stitches. Fast machine speed and slow hand movement will create short stitches. Move quilt sideways, back and forth, in a circular motion, or in a random motion to create the desired designs; do not rotate quilt. Lock stitches at the end of each quilting line.

MAKING A HANGING SLEEVE

Attaching a hanging sleeve to the back of your wall hanging or quilt before the binding is added allows you to display your completed project on a wall.

1. Measure width of quilt top edge and subtract 1". Cut piece of fabric 7" wide by the determined measurement.
2. Press short edges of fabric piece $1/4$" to wrong side; press edges $1/4$" to wrong side again and machine stitch in place.
3. Matching wrong sides, fold piece in half lengthwise to form a tube.
4. Match raw edges and stitch hanging sleeve to center top edge on back of wall hanging.
5. Bind wall hanging, treating the hanging sleeve as part of the backing.
6. Blind stitch bottom of hanging sleeve to backing, taking care not to stitch through to front of quilt.

"The park ranger pointed to a green fabric laced with spidery white and blue lines. 'There are fabrics here we don't have in our quilt, but that doesn't mean they weren't ever there. Our quilt was in that cave a lot of years and some of it just disappeared.'"

—from Lover's Knot

Fig. 26

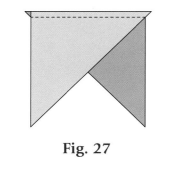

Fig. 27

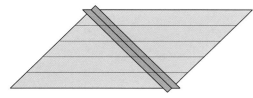

Fig. 28

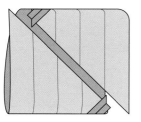

Fig. 29

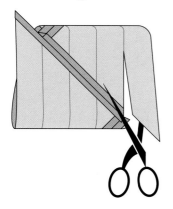

BINDING

Binding encloses the raw edges of your quilt. Because of its stretchiness, bias binding works well for binding projects with curves or rounded corners and tends to lie smooth and flat in any given circumstance. It is also more durable than other types of binding.

MAKING CONTINUOUS BIAS BINDING

Bias strips for binding can simply be cut and pieced to the desired length. However, when a long length of binding is needed, the "continuous" method is quick and accurate.

1. Cut a square from binding fabric the size indicated in the project instructions. Cut square in half diagonally to make 2 triangles.
2. With right sides together and using a $1/4$" seam allowance, sew triangles together (**Fig. 26**); press seam allowance open.
3. On wrong side of fabric, draw lines the width of the binding as specified in the project instructions, usually $2^1/2$" (**Fig. 27**). Cut off any remaining fabric less than this width.
4. With right sides inside, bring short edges together to form a tube; match raw edges so that first drawn line of top section meets second drawn line of bottom section (**Fig. 28**).
5. Carefully pin edges together by inserting pins through drawn lines at the point where drawn lines intersect, making sure the pins go through intersections on both sides. Using a $1/4$" seam allowance, sew edges together. Press seam allowance open.
6. To cut continuous strip, begin cutting along first drawn line (**Fig. 29**). Continue cutting along drawn line around tube.
7. Trim ends of bias strip square.
8. Matching wrong sides and raw edges, press bias strip in half lengthwise to complete binding.

MAKING STRAIGHT-GRAIN BINDING

1. Cut crosswise strips of binding fabric the width called for in project instructions. Sew strips together end-to-end with a diagonal seam to achieve determined length.
2. Matching wrong sides and raw edges, press strip in half lengthwise to complete binding.

ATTACHING BINDING WITH MITERED CORNERS

1. Beginning with one end near center on bottom edge of quilt, lay binding around quilt to make sure that seams in binding will not end up at a corner. Adjust placement if necessary. Matching raw edges of binding to raw edge of quilt top, pin binding to right side of quilt along one edge.
2. When you reach the first corner, mark $1/4$" from corner of quilt top (**Fig. 30**).
3. Beginning approximately 10" from end of binding and using a $1/4$" seam allowance, sew binding to quilt, backstitching at beginning of stitching and at mark (**Fig.31**). Lift needle out of fabric and clip thread.
4. Fold binding as shown in **Figs. 32** and **33** and pin binding to adjacent side, matching raw edges. When you reach the next corner, mark $1/4$" from edge of quilt top.
5. Backstitching at edge of quilt top, sew pinned binding to quilt (**Fig. 34**); backstitch when you reach the next mark. Lift needle out of fabric and clip thread.
6. Continue sewing binding to quilt, stopping approximately 10" from starting point (**Fig. 35**).

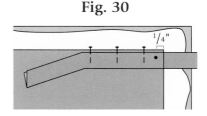

Fig. 30

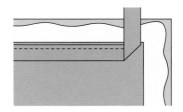

Fig. 31

Fig. 32

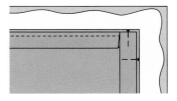

Fig. 33

Fig. 34

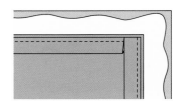

Fig. 35

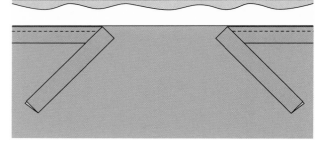

Fig. 36

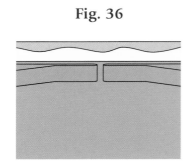

Fig. 37

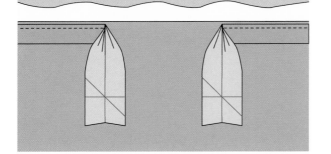

Fig. 38

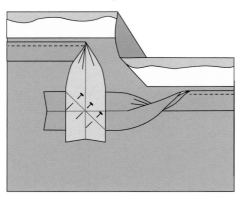

Fig. 39

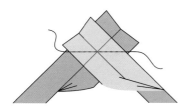

7. Bring beginning and end of binding to center of opening and fold each end back, leaving a $1/4$" space between folds (**Fig. 36**). Finger-press folds.

8. Unfold ends of binding and draw a line across wrong side in finger-pressed crease. Draw a line through the lengthwise pressed fold of binding at same spot to create a cross mark. With edge of ruler at marked cross, line up 45° angle marking on ruler with one long side of binding. Draw a diagonal line from edge to edge. Repeat on remaining end, making sure that the two lines are angled the same way (**Fig. 37**).

9. Matching right sides and diagonal lines, pin binding ends together at right angles (**Fig. 38**).

10. Machine stitch along diagonal line, removing pins as you stitch (**Fig. 39**).

11. Lay binding against quilt to double-check that it is correct length.

12. Trim binding ends, leaving $1/4$" seam allowance; press seam open. Stitch binding to quilt.

13. Trim backing and batting a scant $1/4$" larger than quilt top so that batting and backing will fill the binding when it is folded over to quilt backing.

14. On one edge of quilt, fold binding over to quilt backing and pin pressed edge in place, covering stitching line (**Fig. 40**). On adjacent side, fold binding over, forming a mitered corner (**Fig. 41**). Repeat to pin remainder of binding in place.

15. Blindstitch binding to backing, taking care not to stitch through to front of quilt.

BLIND STITCH

Come up at 1, go down at 2, and come up at 3 (**Fig. 42**). Length of stitches may be varied as desired.

Fig. 40

Fig. 41

Fig. 42

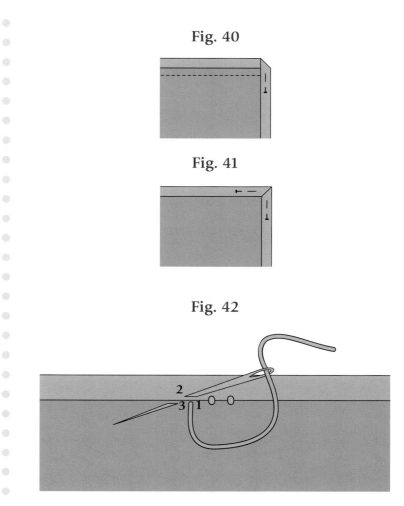

Metric Conversion Chart		
Inches x 2.54 = centimeters (cm)		Yards x .9144 = meters (m)
Inches x 25.4 = millimeters (mm)		Yards x 91.44 = centimeters (cm)
Inches x .0254 = meters (m)		Centimeters x .3937 = inches (")
		Meters x 1.0936 = yards (yd)

Standard Equivalents					
1/8"	3.2 mm	0.32 cm	1/8 yard	11.43 cm	0.11 m
1/4"	6.35 mm	0.635 cm	1/4 yard	22.86 cm	0.23 m
3/8"	9.5 mm	0.95 cm	3/8 yard	34.29 cm	0.34 m
1/2"	12.7 mm	1.27 cm	1/2 yard	45.72 cm	0.46 m
5/8"	15.9 mm	1.59 cm	5/8 yard	57.15 cm	0.57 m
3/4"	19.1 mm	1.91 cm	3/4 yard	68.58 cm	0.69 m
7/8"	22.2 mm	2.22 cm	7/8 yard	80 cm	0.8 m
1"	25.4 mm	2.54 cm	1 yard	91.44 cm	0.91 m

*M*any thanks
go to these ladies for
their beautiful work.

lover's knot

was pieced by Nelwyn Gray and
machine quilted by Julie Schrader.

log cabin

was pieced by Nelwyn Gray and
machine quilted by Julie Schrader.

cactus bloom

was pieced and appliquéd
by Larcie Burnett and machine
quilted by Julie Schrader.

helen's signature blocks

were pieced by Marie Hanley.

production team:

Technical Writers - Lisa Lancaster and Jean Lewis
Editorial Writer - Susan McManus Johnson
Graphic Artist - Dayle Carozza
Photography Stylist - Christy Myers
Staff Designers - Frances Huddleston and Jean Lewis